YOUR KNOWLEDGE HAS VALUE

Neha Sah

Cache working and its performance

GRIN Publishing

Bibliographic information published by the German National Library:

The German National Library lists this publication in the National Bibliography; detailed bibliographic data are available on the Internet at http://dnb.dnb.de .

Imprint:

Copyright © 2013 GRIN Verlag GmbH
Print and binding: Books on Demand GmbH, Norderstedt Germany
ISBN: 978-3-656-55548-3

This book at GRIN:

http://www.grin.com/en/e-book/265630/cache-working-and-its-performance

GRIN - Your knowledge has value

Since its foundation in 1998, GRIN has specialized in publishing academic texts by students, college teachers and other academics as e-book and printed book. The website www.grin.com is an ideal platform for presenting term papers, final papers, scientific essays, dissertations and specialist books.

Visit us on the internet:

http://www.grin.com/

http://www.facebook.com/grincom

http://www.twitter.com/grin_com

CACHE WORKING AND ITS PERFORMANCE

What is Cache?

Cache is a small and fast memory, usually static RAM (SRAM), which is incorporated inside the CPU or placed on a separate chip. The cache stores data which is frequently used in running the programs. By this, the cache increases the speed of accessing the data and the overall performance of the system.

The benefit of using cache is that the CPU does not need to use the motherboard's system to transfer the data. Whenever the CPU has to use the system bus to access the data, this affects the effectiveness of the motherboard by slowing it down. Hence using cache overcomes this problem.

Cache is so effective that the system performance of a fast running CPU with little cache support is less than that of a slow running CPU with more cache support. The cache can be a L1 (incorporated inside the CPU) or L2 (placed in a separate chip). Some systems contain both L1 and L2 cache.

How does Cache increase the CPU Performance?

The improvement in the CPU performance by cache can be explained by the concept of "Locality of Reference". At a time, the processor will be accessing data from a particular region of the memory. This block of memory will be stored in the cache for high speed access, hence increasing the performance.

I can further explain this by using the book analogy:
-Lots of books on my shelf: This is like the main memory.
-A few books on my desk: This is like the L2 cache.
-One book that I'm reading: This is like the L1 cache.

Hits and Misses in the Cache

When the required data that the CPU tries to fetch from the cache is found, then it's called a cache hit and when it's not found then it's called a cache miss. A cache hit transfers the data to the CPU in high speed. However, if there's a cache miss, then the CPU has to access the main memory to fetch the required data. It loads the data from the main memory to the cache which delays the execution of the instructions and lowers the performance.

Cache Mapping

There are various ways by which the main memory is mapped on to the cache:
- Direct Mapping
- Fully Associative Mapping
- Set Associative Mapping

Direct Mapping:
Each memory block is mapped to exactly one cache location. The cache location is decided by the following formula:

Cache Location = (block address) MOD (# of blocks in the cache)

Direct mapping is the most efficient type of mapping scheme; however it does not utilize the cache to the fullest (least effective), as it may not use all the cache lines. There may be a cache miss even when the cache is not full of active lines.

Fully Associative Mapping:
Each memory block is mapped to any random cache location. Here, the cache is fully utilized as none of the cache lines are left unused, but at the expense of speed. The searching of the line which contains a particular memory block is time consuming as the whole of the cache must be scanned to find that block.

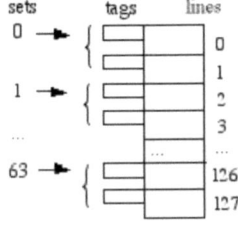

Set Associative Mapping:
Each memory block is mapped to a subset of cache location. The cache location is decided by the following formula:

Set Selection = (block address) MOD (# of sets in the cache)

This is a compromise between direct mapped and fully associative. The cache is divided into a set of tags and the set number is direct mapped from the memory address. In set-associative mapping, when the number of lines per set is *n*, the mapping is called *n*-way associative.

How do we use the memory address to find the block?
We take the following example to explain:
- Main Memory= 16 bits=2^16=64KB
- Cache Memory=8 blocks=128 bits
- Block Size=4 words=16 bytes

Direct Mapping:

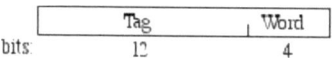

Word: Selects one of the 16 addressable words on the line.
Line: Defines the cache line where the memory will reside.
Tag: It contains an address which is compared with the cache line's 5 bit tag to determine whether it's a hit or a miss.
If there is a miss, we have to replace memory line in that position with the required memory line.

Fully Associative Mapping:

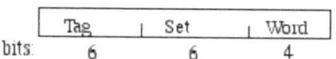

Tag: Identifies one of the 2^{12} = 4096 different memory lines.
All the cache tags have to be searched to find the match of the required tag field. If there's a match, then it's a hit, else, it's a miss and one of the cache lines have to be replaces by the desired memory line.

Set Associative Mapping:

Tag	Set	Word
6	6	4

bits:

Tag: Identifies one of the 2^6 = 64 different memory lines in each of the 2^6 = 64 different "set" values.
Here, each set has 2 lines from where the match of the required memory line has to be searched from. So the whole cache does not need to be searched and the search is confined in those 2 lines.

If there is a miss, one of the 2 lines in that set has to be replaced by the desired memory line.

Replacement Algorithms:

Every time there's a cache miss, the cache has to replace a cache line with the desired memory line. There are various replacements which the cache uses to replace the cache lines:

- Bélády's Algorithm
- Least Recently Used
- Most Recently Used
- Pseudo-LRU
- Random Replacement
- Segmented LRU
- 2-Way Set Associative
- Direct-mapped cache
- Least-Frequently Used
- Low Inter-reference Recency Set
- Adaptive Replacement Cache
- Clock with Adaptive Replacement
- Multi Queue Caching Algorithm

Bélády's Algorithm:
This algorithm removes the data which won't be needed any longer by the CPU. This algorithm is not practically implementable as it is not possible to know which data will not be required unless there are calculations and experiments implemented to compare the effectiveness of the algorithm.

Least Recently Used:
This algorithm replaces the data which is not been accessed in recently. For this, the algorithm keeps a track of which data was used when.
"Age Bits" have to be kept for each cache line and according to this the "Least Recently Used" algorithm is implemented. Age bits are updated every time a cache line is accessed and the age bits of the rest of the cache lines is updated.

Most Recently Used:
This algorithm discards the most recently used data. This is more effective than the Least Recently used algorithm as it has a greater tendency to retain older data.

Pseudo-LRU:
It's an algorithm created to improve the Least Recently Used algorithm. They are used for CPU caches which has an associatively greater than 4, in such case Least Recently Used becomes non-implementable.

Random Replacement:
This algorithm replaces the data in a random manner whenever space is required in the cache memory. As the replacement is random, there is no need for keeping any kind of track on the data (like in LRU). Such algorithms are used in processes which analyses complex chemical reactions (stochastic simulation).

Segmented LRU:
SLRU is an advancement to LRU. It's divided into 2 segments-(i) Probationary Segment & (ii) Protected Segment. In each of the segments, the lines are arranged from most to least recently used data. Data from hits and misses are kept at the end of protected segment and probationary segment respectively. The size of protected segment is limited. Migration of a line from the probationary segment to the protected segment may force the migration of the LRU line in the protected segment to the most recently used (MRU) end of the probationary segment, giving this line another chance to be accessed before being replaced.

What happens in Cache Read and Writes?
Cache read does not affect the content of the cache. Data is simply accessed and there is no modification made on that data.

Cache write, however, has to be dealt in a different manner. As writing a data will obviously change and modify the already present data and its utmost important to keep the data consistent between the cache and the main memory.

There are 2 ways by which the cache and the main memory are kept consistent:
- Write-back cache
- Write-through cache

Write-back Cache:
The data is first modified in the cache and that modification is not made in the main memory immediately. The main memory is updated only when the cache blocks has to be replaced.

It's difficult to implement write-back cache as the locations where there was data written has to be kept track of. They are marked as *dirty lines,* and then these lines are written back to the main memory.

A read miss in write-back cache leads to two memory accesses- one to write the replaced data from the cache to the main memory and the second one to fetch the required data from the main memory to the cache.

Write-through Cache:
In this type of cache, the data in the cache and the main memory is kept constantly synchronous. Whenever there is any modification in the cache, that modification is instantly made in the main memory.

Dealing with Write-Misses:
There are two ways by which a write miss can be handled:
- Write-Allocate
- No-Write Allocate

Write-Allocate:
Its working is same like the read miss. The data at the write-miss location is fetched in the cache, followed by a write hit operation.
So in other words, the data block is written in the cache, it is updated and then anticipated for any further use of the block.

No-Write Allocate:
Here, the data is not fetched in the cache. It's updated directly in the main memory. In this approach, only system reads are cached.
Only the contents of the main memory are modified, the contents of the cache remains unchanged.

Improving the Performance of Cache:
To improve the performance of the cache, the first and the foremost reduction to make is cache misses.

There are three types of cache misses:
1. Compulsory
2. Capacity
3. Conflict

Compulsory:
On the first access of the cache block, there is a cache miss; this is called as compulsory miss, the block has to be brought to the cache. It is also called as cold start misses or first reference misses.

Capacity:
When the program working set is much larger than the capacity of the cache size, then the cache bocks have to be replaced because there is not enough space for the whole data which is required in the execution of the program.

Conflict:
Direct mapped or set associative mapped caches usually face this problem when several blocks are mapped to the same set of the block. This type of miss is also called as interference misses or collision misses.

How can we improve the Cache Performance?
There are basically 3 ways to improve the cache performance:
1. Reduce Miss Rate
2. Reduce Cache Miss Penalty
3. Reduce Cache Hit Time

Miss Rate Reduction Techniques:
- Increased Cache Capacity
- Larger block size
- Higher Associativity
- Victim caches
- Hardware pre-fetching of instructions and data
- Pseudo-associative Caches
- Compiler-controlled pre-fetching
- Compiler optimizations

Cache Miss Penalty Reduction Techniques:
- Giving priority to read misses over writes
- Sub-block placement
- Early restart and critical word first
- Non-blocking caches
- Second-level cache (L2)

Cache Hit Time Reduction Techniques:
- Small and simple caches
- Avoiding address translation during cache indexing
- Pipelining writes for fast write hits

I'll explain a few concepts in detail here:

Larger block size: If the cache size is increased then a larger block of the main memory (according to the concept of "Locality of Reference") can be brought into the cache. This gives more chances of hits and increasing the performance of the cache.

Victim Caches: Data discarded from cache is placed in an added small buffer (victim cache). On a cache miss check victim cache for data before going to main memory.

Hardware pre-fetching of Instructions and Data: Pre-fetch instructions and data before they are needed by the CPU either into cache or into an external buffer.

Compiler Optimizations:
- *Reorder procedure* in memory to reduce conflict misses.
- *Merging Arrays*: Improve spatial locality by single array of compound elements vs. 2 arrays.
- *Loop Interchange*: Change nesting of loops to access data in the order stored in memory.
- *Loop Fusion*: Combine 2 or more independent loops that have the same looping and some variables overlap.
- *Blocking*: Improve temporal locality by accessing "blocks" of data repeatedly vs. going down whole columns or rows.

Sub-block Replacement: Divide a cache block frame into a number of sub-blocks.
- Include a valid bit per sub-block of cache block frame to indicate validity of sub-block.
  – Originally used to reduce tag storage (fewer block frames).
- No need to load a full block on a miss just the needed sub-block

Early restart and critical word first:
- Early restart: As soon as the requested word of the block arrives, send it to the CPU and let the CPU continue execution.
- Critical Word First: Request the missed word first from memory and send it to the CPU as soon as it arrives.
- Let the CPU continue execution while filling the rest of the words in the block.
- Also called wrapped fetch and requested word first.
- Generally useful only for caches with large block sizes.
- Programs with a high degree of spatial locality tend to require a number of sequential words, and may not benefit by early restart.

Non-blocking Cache: Non-blocking cache or lockup-free cache allows data cache to continue to supply cache hits during the processing of a miss:
- Requires an out-of-order execution CPU.
- "Hit under miss" reduces the effective miss penalty by working during misses vs. ignoring CPU requests.
- "Hit under multiple miss" or "miss under miss" may further lower the effective miss penalty by overlapping multiple misses.
- Significantly increases the complexity of the cache controller as there can be multiple outstanding memory accesses.
- Requires multiple memory banks to allow multiple memory access requests.

Avoiding address translation during cache indexing:
Send virtual address to cache: Called Virtually Addressed Cache or just Virtual Cache vs. Physical Cache

- Every time process is switched logically the cache must be flushed; otherwise it will return false hit
- Cost is time to flush + "compulsory" misses from empty cache
- Dealing with aliases (sometimes called synonyms); Two different virtual addresses map to same physical address
- I/O must interact with cache, so need virtual address

Solution to aliases:

- HW guarantees covers index field & direct mapped, they must be unique; this is called page coloring

Solution to cache flushes:

- Add process identifier tag that identifies a process as well as address within process: can't get a hit if wrong process